ABOVE: *A gathering of herbalists from all ages. Dioscorides is seated centrally, with Pliny at his right hand, holding a book. On his left is an Arab herbalist holding a sprig of a plant. Twelfth-century writings, thought to be originally in Arabic and attributed by others to Serapion the Younger, did a lot to distribute knowledge from the Arab world into Europe. Peter Schoeffer, 1485*

First published 2022
This edition © Wooden Books Ltd 2025

Published by Wooden Books Ltd.
Glastonbury, Somerset.
www.woodenbooks.com

British Library Cataloguing in Publication Data
Ponting, C.
*British Wild Flowers*

A CIP catalogue record for this book
may be obtained from the British Library.

ISBN-10: 1-907155-42-2
ISBN-13: 978-1-907155-42-0

Designed and typeset in Glastonbury, UK.
Printed in India on FSC® certified papers by
Quarterfold Printabilities Pvt. Ltd.

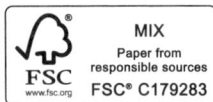

WOODEN BOOKS

# BRITISH WILD
# FLOWERS

## THEIR NAMING AND FOLKLORE

*Gerald Ponting*

To the memory of my mother, Nellie Ponting, who encouraged my love of wild flowers from an early age and also to the memory of Miss Marion Darke. She heard my name on BBC Children's Hour Nature Parliament as an 8-year-old who had sent in a query about wild flowers. She gave me her late father's copy of 'Flowers of the Field' and appointed herself an honorary aunt. I also owe a huge debt to authors of floras, herbals and other works on wild flowers, especially to Geoffrey Grigson, whose books 'An Englishman's Flora' and 'A Dictionary of English Plant Names' were invaluable in my research. Thanks go to Martin Rand for his many helpful suggestions, also to Sandra Horn, to Anthony Light and to my wife Elizabeth. A big thank you to John Martineau who has laboured long and hard to make this into such an attractive book.

ABOVE: Illustration from the title page of the Grete Herball, England's first illustrated herbal, printed in London in 1526 by Peter Treveris. Wild clover and other flowers in the foreground are framed by a pair of mandrakes, while fruit and flowers are gathered in the background. TITLE PAGE: Violet.

MARSH MARIGOLD   CORN MARIGOLD

ABOVE: *When is a* **MARIGOLD** *not a* **MARIGOLD**? *The* **CORN MARIGOLD** *once made golden swathes across cultivated fields, so was described as 'an yll wede' in a sixteenth-century Book of Husbandry. Formerly just known as* **GOLDS**, *its full name comes from association with garden marigolds, flowers associated with the Virgin Mary and used at Lady Day festivals. Ironically, the cultivated* **MARY-GOLD** *may have been linked with the Virgin to distinguish it from the useless* **GOLDS** *of farmland.*

# INTRODUCTION

THE **KINGCUP** is a familiar yellow springtime flower, named as a king-sized buttercup. Its other familiar name, **MARSH MARIGOLD**, clearly comes from the plant's habitat in damp marshy meadows and from a comparison with the unrelated **CORN MARIGOLD** (*Glebionis segetum*). It has been known as **GOLDILOCKS** in Somerset, as **HALCUP** in Hampshire, as **JOHN GEORGES** in Northamptonshire, as **YELLOW BOOTS** in Cheshire, and so on across the country. In 1958 Geoffrey Grigson, having consulted dialect dictionaries and other sources, listed alternative local names for the common flowers of the countryside. For the Marsh Marigold he recorded no less than ninety-one names. The European total would be much higher. This emphasises the fact that botanists need an internationally accepted name for each plant—in this case *Caltha palustris*.

The familiar names of our wild flowers originate from many sources, some from Old English as spoken before 1100. Others have been adopted from French, German and other modern languages.

Writers of herbals from the 1480s onwards, consulting classical texts, often transferred Greek or Latin names onto British plants (*as explained on page 8*). They also invented English names, sometimes based on the name of a person whom they wished to commemorate. Some names are based on legends or other stories.

A name may indicate the usefulness of a plant, often but not always its use as a medicinal or culinary herb. Flowering plants have also been named on the basis of their time of flowering, their habitat, their pattern of growth, or their similarity to some other plant.

# CLASSICAL HERBALISTS
## Dioscorides and Pliny the Elder

---

The first person to produce a written systematic study of plants was Pedanius Dioscorides [40–90 AD], a Greek, living in the Roman Province of Cilicia, now in southern Turkey (*see frontispiece*). Although written in Greek, Dioscorides' book is best known by its Latin name, *De Materia Medica*, and it mainly deals with the uses of plants in healing afflictions of the body. Copied, translated into other languages and laboriously copied by hand again, it became the standard herbal, at least across Europe, for the next thousand years and more.

Around the same time, the Roman encyclopedist Pliny the Elder [23–79 AD] was gathering information from many sources for his huge *Naturalis Historia*, which eventually ran to 37 volumes (or scrolls), of which 16 were devoted to plants. Myth and superstition took equal place with facts, while some ideas verged on fantasy (*see Celandines, p.24*). Nevertheless, like *De Materia Medica*, his material was copied and recopied; over 200 medieval versions survive to this day. Pliny died aged 56 when, curious to the last about natural phenomena, he decided to have a closer look at the eruption which destroyed Pompeii.

THIS PAGE AND FACING: *Illustrations from a sixth-century copy of Dioscorides' De Materia Medica, which survives in Vienna. It is not known whether these pictures are copies from the first-century original.*

# THE RENAISSANCE HERBALISTS
## *the dawn of printed herbals*

Johannes Gutenberg's invention of the printing press in the 1450s, in Mainz, Germany, revolutionised the dissemination of information, with a cultural significance at least as great as the development of the modern internet. The new technology spread rapidly, with printers quickly turning their attention to classical texts, including herbals.

A printed version of Pliny's great work appeared in 1469 and of Dioscorides' in 1478. Peter Schoeffer, a former apprentice of Gutenberg, published his popular and frequently reprinted *Herbarius Latinus* in 1484. Although probably conceived as a printed book, the plant descriptions came from earlier manuscript sources.

Over subsequent centuries, botanical writers in northern Europe compiled new herbals which drew too heavily on classical writings. Thus, in herbals by Otto Brunfels (Germany, 1530), Henry Lyte (England, 1578) and others, we find local plants equated with descriptions of those found in Mediterranean regions, the authors seemingly unaware that flora differs between cooler and warmer climes.

Examples of the transfer of Classical names to (possibly quite different) northern plants by Renaissance herbalists are **MILKWORT** (*see opposite page*), **HAWKWEED** (*p.12*), **LOOSESTRIFE** (*p.14*), and **AGRIMONY** (*opposite, and p.16*).

4

**Absintheü        wermut**
Absinthcü est calidü in primo gdu et sicci in sedo et habet pontücis. amarüsimi sapocé et debt col ligim sue veris in umbra exsiccari et p änü ser

**Camomilla        Camillen**
Camomilla est calida et sicca in primo habet virtutē mollificatoi et dissoluentē. frondes et flores sunt ej lis virtutis. Et aqua decoctionis ej cü arthmesia cü

**Agrimonia        Odermenich**
Agrimonia est calida et sicca in sedo. Dessic̄co entdins euis euisdlaia et poul.a veris. gete sullā blomcü cü vino veteri vt ad palitus- illo mō sit

**Luppulus        Hopfen**
Luppulus est calidum et siccu in primo gradu ve frigiditatem declinans. Est autem sapoꝰis color calidoes et exsigantius instanmaciōū et lenitiuꝰ.

RIGHT: **MILKWORT** (Polygala vulgaris). *Dioscorides said that a plant called polugalon was believed to make milk more abundant – referring no doubt to grazing sheep and goats. A tiny flower of the English chalk downlands, usually blue but sometimes pink, was known as* **SHEPHERD'S THYME** *in Wiltshire. Lyte made an assumption that it was the same as Greek polugalon, so invented the name* **MILKWORT** – *and promptly prescribed it for nursing human mothers. (Greek polugalon and Latin polygala both mean 'much milk.')*

Milkwort

# THE DOCTRINE OF SIGNATURES
*the apparent is the bridge to the real*

How is a pretty blue flower like the **FIELD SCABIOUS** (*Knautia arvensis*) related to the unpleasant skin disease scabies? Both derive their names ultimately from the Latin verb, *scabo* – to scratch. The unopened buds and the dried seed heads both have a 'scabby' appearance. Therefore, preparations of the plant were frequently used by the old apothecaries to cure scabies and other itching conditions of the skin.

This idea, fantastic though it may seem to us, was not only the basis for the name of this plant, but also the foundation of a whole theory of medicine. The idea was introduced by Paracelsus around 1530 and developed into a fully-fledged system by Giambattista Porta in his *Phytognomonica* (Plant Indicators) of 1588. Heart-shaped fruits such as peaches were considered effective in the treatment of heart conditions, while walnut kernels cured brain diseases. Because the flat green 'thallus' of a **LIVERWORT**, a non-flowering plant, is divided into lobes, like the lobes of the human liver, it should be effective in treating liver diseases. Other examples include **CELANDINES** (*see p.24*) and **ORCHIDS** (*see p.34*).

Liverwort

Scabious

St John's Wort

LEFT: **LUNGWORT** (Pulmonaria officinalis), originally a garden plant, is now naturalised throughout Britain. As its spotty leaves resemble a diseased lung, it was considered a treatment for lung disorders. The flowers change from pink to blue, hence its local name **SOLDIERS AND SAILORS**.

LEFT: **ST JOHN'S WORT** (Hypericum spp). William Coles wrote: 'The little holes whereof the leaves of Saint John's Wort are full, doe resemble all the pores of the skin and therefore it is profitable for all hurts and wounds that can happen thereunto'. Today, preparations are advised for depression. With its yellow flowers it was called **PENNY JOHN** in Norfolk.

LEFT: Giambattista Porta's DOCTRINE OF SIGNATURES. Porta believed that God had dropped a hint (or placed a 'signature') on plant parts which would be useful in the treatment of disease or injury. This illustration from his Phytognomonica suggests that 'scaly' plants such as **PINE CONES**, **KNAPWEED BUDS**, **CATKINS** and **LILY BULBS** could be used to treat scaly conditions of the skin. The snake and the fish are presumably included as examples of scaly skin!

# GERARD'S HERBALL
*the first among equals*

---

John Gerard, in his Holborn garden, cultivated over 1000 species of plants, many of them new and exotic, including the potato. His popular 1597 *Herball* started as an English translation of a 1554 Dutch herbal by Rembert Dodoens. Was Gerard acquainted with Shakespeare? Both were eminent men, and the Bard's lodging was not far from Holborn. Many phrases in the plays show Shakespeare's interest in plants and gardening (*see pages 22, 26 and 30-35*)—perhaps he had a copy of the *Herball* on his bookshelf—and both had a way with words:

Gerard describes the Dandelion (Taraxacum spp.) as "*a floure ... of colour yellow, and sweet in smell, which is turned into a round downy blowball that is carried away by the wind*". The name comes from the French *dentes de lion* (lion's teeth, from the shape of the leaves). Local names of Piss-a-bed and Pee-a-bed refer to the diuretic properties of the stem sap (*see also page 12*).

Gerard also invented new names for many plants. Of our wild white **CLEMATIS** (*Clematis vitalba, illustrated right*), he wrote that it was a plant *"decking and adorning waies and hedges, where people travel, and thereupon I have named it Travellers' Ioie"*. Brought up in Cheshire, he seems to have been unaware of the popular southern name of **OLD MAN'S BEARD**, referring to the fluffy seeds which, like those of the dandelion, are spread by the wind.

1 *Cardamine.* Cuckow floures.

2 *Cardamine altera.* Ladies-smocke.

3 *Saluia Indica.* Indian Sage.

4 *Saluia Alpina.* Mountaine Sage.

‡ 3 *Cardamine altera flore pleno.* Double floured Lady-smocke.

4 *Cardamine Trifolia.* Three leaued Lady-smocke.

2 ‡ *Saluia Cretica pomifera,* Apple-bearing Sage of Candy,

‡ *Saluia Cretica non pomifera,* Candy Sage without Apples.

1 *Digitalis purpurea.* Purple Fox-gloues.

2 *Digitalis alba.* White Fox-gloues.

3 *Viola martia purpurea multiplex.* The double garden purple Violet.

5 *Viola martia lutea.* Yellow Violets.

‡ 3 *Digitalis lutea.* Yellow Fox-gloues.

‡ 4 *Digitalis ferruginea.* Dusky Fox-gloues.

*Taraxacum officinale* Dandelion

Selected pages
from Gerard's
Herbal of 1597.
The translation
was started by
Dr Robert Priest
before Gerard took
over the work.

# COMMEMORATING BOTANISTS
## *the art of coining Linnaean names*

---

**RED BARTSIA** (*Odontites vernus*) is an inconspicuous plant, with dull red flowers, growing among grasses and partly parasitic on them. Too insignificant to have acquired any dialect names, it takes its English name from the former name of its genus. Carl Linnaeus [1707-1778] named it *Bartsia* after Johann Bartsch, a Swedish botanist who was badly affected by the tropical climate during an expedition to Dutch Suriname. He died there in 1738, aged 29.

Linnaeus' binomial system, *Genus* followed by *species*, is still used today by scientists to name plants and animals—and incorporating the names of botanists into the Linnaean names of plants has long been a common practice, with some of these even being adopted as common names.

The genus **DAHLIA** (*right*) was named in 1791, when the first specimens were received from Mexico, to commemorate Andreas Dahl (another Swedish botanist, who had died two years previously). Other Mexican specimens, e.g. **ZINNIA**, were named after Bavarian botanist, Johann Zinn.

Dahlia

**RED BARTSIA**, *taxonomy:*
KINGDOM: *Plantae*
CLADE: *Angiospermae*
ORDER: *Lamiales*
FAMILY: *Orobranchaceae*
GENUS: *Odontites*
SPECIES: *O. vernus*
(*Odontities, for 'toothache';*
*vernus for 'spring-flowering'.*)

**YELLOW-RATTLE** (Rhinanthus minor) *is semi-parasitic on grasses and legumes. Its seeds' rattle told farmers that hay was ready to cut (while reducing the crop). Planting Yellow-rattle in a wild flower meadow increases biodiversity by restricting grass growth, allowing other species to thrive.*

**BROOMRAPE** (Orobanche minor), *has no leaves or chlorophyll so is totally parasitic. It feeds from the roots of broom, gorse and other plants (e.g.* **CLOVER** *here, as shown). Rape is an old word for turnip, implying that the plant has a swollen root.*

**BROOM** (Cytisus scoparius), *left, was used for sweeping the floor and this has given us the word 'broom' for a brush.*

**BUTCHER'S BROOM** (Ruscus aculeatus), *right, was used by Victorian butchers to decorate their Christmas sirloins with its red berry-bearing twigs. Aculeatus is Latin for 'prickly'.*

Broom

Butcher's
Broom

# DANDELION-LIKE FLOWERS
## stars within a family of stars

---

**DANDELIONS** (*Taraxacum spp.*) belong to the *Asteraceae* family, formerly called *Compositae* because they have composite flowers. Each 'flower' is actually a group of much smaller flowers, a flower-head or capitulum, where each 'petal' is a complete flower. Each 'floret' consists of five tiny petals fused together, with the male stamens forming a tube around the female style. Tiny hairs at the base form a pappus, which matures into the downy seed 'parachute' (*see drawings below*).

*Taraxacum* is a very variable genus; specialist knowledge is needed to distinguish between hundreds of species and sub-species. The same is true of the **HAWKWEEDS** (*Hieracium spp.*). In 1568, Turner identified our Hawkweeds with Pliny's *hieracion* (from *hierax*, Greek for hawk); he had written that hawks tear it apart '*… and wet their eyes with its juice, so dispelling dimness of sight …*'.

**FOX-AND-CUBS** (*Pilosella aurantiaca*) is named from several small flower-heads surrounding a larger one, all the intense colour of fox fur.

The type genus of the family is *Aster*, from the Greek for star. Michaelmas Daisies (*Symphyotrichum* but formerly *Aster*) are North American plants which escaped from gardens and became naturalised in Britain. Other members of *Asteraceae* include Corn Marigold (*p.1*), Knapweed (*p.20*), Daisies (*p.28*), Thistles (*p.38*), Burdock (*p.36*), Butterbur (*p.47*), Ragwort (*p.38*), Yarrow (*p.44*), Fleabane (*p.47*), Colt's-foot (*p.49*) and many more.

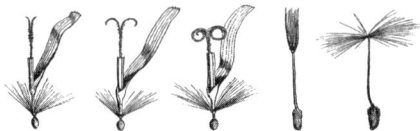

| Michaelmas Daisy | Hawkbit | Hawk's-beards | Hawkweed |

**HAWKBITS** (Leonotodon spp.), **HAWK'S-BEARDS** (Crepis spp.) **HAWKWEEDS** (Hieracium spp.) and **MOUSE-EAR-HAWKWEEDS** (Pilosella spp.) *have smaller Dandelion-like flowers.*

Groundsel

Tansy

*FAR LEFT: In the seventh century* **GROUNDSEL** (Senecio vulgaris) *was* **GUNDESUILGE**, *a swallower of matter or pus and used as a cure for watering of the eyes. Later, it was* **GRUNDESWYLIGE** *the 'ground-swallower,' as it can rapidly take over waste ground.*

*LEFT:* **TANSY** (Tanacetun vulgare), *or* **GOLDEN BUTTONS** *in Somerset, has long been grown or gathered for varied herbal properties. Culpepper advised 'Let those Women that desire Children love this Herb, 'tis their best Companion, their Husband excepted'. Its spicy aroma was used to repel flies, e.g. by rubbing it on meat.*

# Loosestrifes & Pimpernels
## *nothing to do with saxifrages*

---

**YELLOW LOOSESTRIFE** (*Lysimachia vulgaris*) was given its name in 1548 by William Turner, who took it to be the plant known by Dioscorides (*see p.6*) as **LUSIMAKHEIOS** *'deliverance from strife'*. Pliny expanded on this: *'placed on the yoke of inharmonious oxen it will restrain their quarrelling'*. Thus you lose the strife!

Turner named **PURPLE-LOOSESTRIFE** (*Lythrum salicaria*) on the basis of a superficial similarity to the Yellow—both have tall flowering spikes and lanceolate leaves, but they are not related. In Millais's painting of Ophelia's suicide, Purple-loosestrife represents Shakespeare's 'long purples' (*see p.34*). Many herbal properties were claimed for it—a treatment for diarrhoea or for dysentery, a gargle for sore throats, or an eye lotion said to be superior to **EYEBRIGHT** (*p.42*).

**YELLOW PIMPERNEL** (*Lysimachia nemorum*) is a much lower-growing plant than Yellow Loosestrife. **SCARLET PIMPERNEL** (*L. arvensis*), which sometimes has blue flowers, is a common arable weed. All belong to the Primrose family (*Primulaceae*). The Old French name *pimprenelle* rightly belongs to **BURNET-SAXIFRAGE** (*Pimpinella saxifraga*) rather than to the Pimpernels. In another confusion, this plant is unrelated to the true **SAXIFRAGES** (*Saxifraga spp.*).

Burnet-saxifrage

Yellow Loosestrife

Purple-loosestrife

Yellow Pimpernel

Scarlet Pimpernel

Opposite-leaved Golden Saxifrage

LEFT: *The leaves and tiny flowers of* **OPPOSITE-LEAVED GOLDEN SAXIFRAGE** (Chrysosplenium oppositifolium) *are both pale yellow, leading to the local name of* **BUTTERED EGGS**. *Unlike most Saxifrages which grow in rock crevices, it prefers damp shady areas. The name comes from Latin* saxum, *rock, and* frangere, *to break, as they were thought to be effective in breaking up human gall-stones.*

ABOVE LEFT: **SCARLET PIMPERNEL** *flowers close up in afternoons or wet weather, leading to names of* **JOHN-GO-TO-BED-AT-NOON** *or* **SHEPHERD'S WEATHERGLASS**. *The flower was the symbol and the nom de guerre of the eponymous protagonist in Baroness Orczy's 1905 novel.*

# NAMES FROM ANCIENT GREEK
## *long-billed birds, cataracts and rainbows*

---

The **WOOD ANEMONE** (*Anemone nemorosa*) has white petals, occasionally with pale purple streaking. The name derives from *anemos*, Greek for wind, and it has been called the **WIND-FLOWER**. Ovid wrote of them: '*Yet does their beauty but a while remain, For their light-hanging petals, but weakly plac'd, The winds, from which their name they borrow, blast.*' The connection with wind may be that it flowers in windy March weather, or perhaps the Greeks adapted the earlier Aramaic name of *na'aman*, meaning 'pleasantness'.

The tall narrow yellow flower spikes of **AGRIMONY** (*Agrimonia eupatoria*) are common on rough grassland. Its name comes from the Greek *argemon* 'a cataract in the eye'. Dioscorides gave the name to a poppy used to treat this condition (*p.5*). European herbalists transferred the name to our Agrimony, despite its total lack of resemblance to a poppy. Chaucer recommended infusions of the leaves for all wounds and for a bad back. It is also known as **CHURCH STEEPLES**, **FAIRY'S WAND** and **STICKLEWORT**.

Wood Anemone

Agrimony

Yellow Iris

LEFT: *The statuesque* **YELLOW IRIS** (*Iris pseudacorus*) *of marshes and riversides is also called* **YELLOW FLAG** *and was probably Shakespeare's* **FLOWER-DE-LUCE** (*fleur-de-lis in French*). '*Yellow Iris,'however, is a misnomer, as the Greek word 'iris' means 'rainbow' and was applied to irises whose petals had iridescent hues, since Iris was the goddess of the rainbow.*

RIGHT: *Violet-flowering* **MEADOW CRANESBILL** (*Geranium pratense*) *is one of many Geranium species in the English countryside. Its seed-head resembles the long bill of a crane. The genus name comes from the Greek geranos, 'crane'. Cultivated 'geraniums' belong to the South African genus Pelargonium; from pelargos, 'stork', another long billed bird.*

Meadow Cranesbill

Green Alkanet

LEFT: **GREEN ALKANET** (*Pentaglottis sempervirens*) *is named from its similarity to* **DYER'S ALKANET** (*Alkanna tinctoria*), *a continental species. In turn, that derives its name from the Arabic al-henna – a red dye derived from the roots, used among other things to colour the liquid in thermometers. Green Alkanet does not provide a dye and would be better called Evergreen Alkanet, as its flowers are blue.*

# BLUEBELLS & HAREBELLS
## *daffodils and other confusions too*

---

The earliest record of the name **BLUEBELL** being used for *Hyacinthoides non-scripta* was in 1794. Prior to this, the lovely bell-shaped blue flower (*shown below*), growing so profusely in many English woodlands, was known as **CROWTOES, LILY-LEAVED STARRY HYACINTH**, or **HAREBELL**. The plant has a magical aura; a lone person picking a flower might be led away by the pixies, a myth preserved in the old playground singing game *In and Out the Dusty Bluebells*. Sticky sap extracted from the stems was concentrated into a glue, used to fix the feathers on arrows. Once picked in huge numbers, today it is threatened by climate change.

In his 1597 *Herball*, Gerard's 'Harebell' is the plant we today call the Bluebell. In Shakespeare's *Cymbeline*, when Arviragus talks of '*fairest flowers*', he includes the '*pale primrose*' with the '*azur'd harebell*' – our Bluebell was probably in the Bard's mind. To add to the confusion, *Campanula rotundifolia* (*right*) is today called **HAREBELL** in England, but Bluebell in Scotland. In Somerset it has been called **BLUEBELLS OF SCOTLAND**. The name does not derive from 'hair-bell' (due to the very fine stems), but instead from it sharing its grassland habitat with hares. The hare has long been thought of as a witch's animal so the plant has also been called **WITCH BELLS** or **WITCHES' THIMBLES**, so it too has magical connections.

Bluebell          Harebell

Wild
Daffodil

Bog
Asphodel

ABOVE: *Wordsworth's famous 'host of golden daffodils' probably refer to the* **WILD DAFFODIL** (*Narcissus pseudonarcissus*). *It makes glorious swathes of yellow in woods and meadows where it is still found. Also known as* **DAFF-A-DOWN-DILLY**, *it was named* **AFFODIL** *in medieval times due to a confusion with the* **ASPHODEL**, *the only common British species of which is the small yellow-flowered* **BOG ASPHODEL** (*Narthecium ossifragum*).

Wood Spurge

Bugle

LEFT: **WOOD SPURGE** (*Euphorbia amygdaloides*) *flowers in abundance in cut coppices, its lush green growth acting as a natural foil to Bluebells. The strange green flowers gave rise to the Somerset name of* **DEVIL'S CUP AND SAUCER**. *It is a 'purging herb', a natural laxative.*

LEFT: *The little blue flowers of* **BUGLE** (*Ajuga reptans*) *were likened to lustrous glass beads once sewn as ornaments on clothes – not to musical instruments.*

# BACHELOR'S BUTTONS
*the divination of romance*

---

The name Bachelor's Buttons has been applied to at least fifteen different wild flowers, from **RED CAMPION** (*Silene dioica, opposite*) as far afield as Devon and Cumberland, to **STITCHWORT** (*p.46*) in Suffolk; **BUTTERCUPS** (*p.27*), **PERIWINKLE** (*p.33*), **BURDOCK** (*p.36*) and **TANSY** (*p.13*), all in Somerset; **DEVILS BIT SCABIOUS** (*opposite*) in Hampshire; and **MARSH MARIGOLD** in many counties (*p.1*).

The name conjures up an image of young unmarried countrymen wearing these flowers in their buttonholes. In fact, in the 16th century, maidens placed several Red Campion flowers under their aprons, each one given the name of some eligible young man. A little later, the one which opened most fully would indicate her most favoured suitor.

John Clare's 1827 poem *May* describes a similar method. As '*young girls whispered things of love*' they used the prominent florets of **KNAPWEED** (*Centaurea nigra*) to predict their sweethearts:

> … *They pull the little blossom threads*
> *From out the knapweeds button heads*
> *And put the husk wi many a smile*
> *In their white bosoms for awhile*
> *Who if they guess aright the swain*
> *That loves sweet fancys trys to gain*
> *Tis said that ere its lain an hour*
> *Twill blossom wi a second flower.*

Greater
Knapweed

Red Campion            Sea Campion

*ABOVE:* **RED CAMPION**. *The origin of the word 'campion' is uncertain – maybe it was a flower used to make garlands for champions.* **SEA CAMPION** *(Silene uniflora), growing on cliffs and shingle beaches, attracts night-flying moths with bright white petals and attractive scent. Other members of the genus Silene are called* **CATCHFLYS** *from the sticky secretions of the plants.*

*RIGHT:* **DEVIL'S-BIT SCABIOUS** *(Succisa pratensis) This innocent-looking little blue-flowering scabious gets its name from the herbalists' medieval Latin, morsus diaboli. The devil has bitten off its root to lessen its curative powers. Culpepper recommended it for all kinds of ailments. When Geoffrey Grigson collected local English names for wild flowers in the 1970s, he found almost 60 names related to the devil, from* **DEVIL'S CHERRIES** *for* **DEADLY NIGHTSHADE** *(p.56) to* **DEVIL'S GUTS** *for* **BINDWEED** *(p.55).*

*FACING PAGE: Pink-flowering* **GREATER KNAPWEED** *(Centaurea scabiosa). Similar* **COMMON KNAPWEED** *(Centaurea nigra), found in rough grassland, is known as* **HARDHEADS**, *due to the solidity of the bud and young seedhead. 'Knap' or 'knop' means 'head' in German & French.*

Devil's bit
Scabious

# Cowslips & Primroses
## Primula veris & Primula vulgaris

Primroses and Cowslips are well-loved yellow flowers of springtime, and their names were formerly used interchangeably. In 1629 John Parkinson distinguished them thus: '*I doe therefore call those onely Primroses that carry one flower upon a stalke, and those Cowslips, that bear many flowers upon a stalk*'. Parkinson, Botanist Regius Primarius to Charles I, was one of the first to describe plants for ornamental as well as herbal uses.

The **PRIMROSE** had many practical uses. Gerard writes that '*Primrose Tea … is famous for curing the phrensie*' (nervous disorders). The name comes from the Latin *prima rosa*, the first rose ('rose' in the loose sense of 'flower'), the primrose considered the first bloom of spring.

Because each **COWSLIP** petal bears a red spot, concoctions of the plant were said to clear up spotty skin. A country wine made from Cowslips was said to be soporific. Cowslip flowers are grouped on the stem, a little like a bunch of keys, giving rise to the old Somerset name of **ST PETER'S KEYS**. 'Cowslip' comes from the Old English *cowslop*, meaning cow-dung, as it grows in cow meadows!

**WOOD AVENS** (*Geum urbanum, shown right*) and the related **WATER AVENS** (*G. rivale*) are both members of the Rose Family. 'Avens' derives from medieval Latin, *avancia*. It is also known as **HERB BENNETT**, *herba benedicta*, 'the blessed herb'; its roots have the scent and flavour of cloves.

Herb Bennett

Primrose       Cowslip       Oxlip

*ABOVE:* **PRIMROSE**, **COWSLIP** *and Oxlip. In The Winter's Tale, Shakespeare included 'bold oxlips' in Perdita's 'flowers of spring'. The* **FALSE OXLIP** *is a natural hybrid between Cowslip and Primrose (P. veris x vulgaris). The true* **OXLIP** *(Primula elatior), is found only in East Anglia.*

Mignonette       Crosswort

*LEFT:* **MIGNONETTE** *(Reseda lutea) has spikes of greenish-yellow flowers. Like Cowslips it prefers calcareous soils. Since Neolithic times it has been used to make a yellow dye called weld. The name means 'little darling' in French.*

**CROSSWORT** *(Cruciata laevipes), also found on chalky ground, is named from the botanical Latin cruciata planta, referring to the cross-shaped arrangement of four tiny leaves at each level around the stem, with groups of little pale yellow flowers above them. Also called* **SMOOTH BEDSTRAW**.

# THE CELANDINES
## *Chelidonium majus & Ranunculus ficaria*

---

The two Celandines are unrelated and have little in common apart from their yellow flowers. The **GREATER CELANDINE** is a species of **POPPY** while the **LESSER CELANDINE** is a member of the **BUTTERCUP** Family. They gain their name from an association with swallows, *chelidonia* in the Greek, which appears in Pliny's *Natural History* (*see page 2*): '*It is by the aid of chelidonia that the swallow restores the sight of the young birds in the nest and even, as some persons will have it, when the eyes have been plucked out*'. Pliny also gives a second, more mundane, explanation: the time of flowering corresponds to the arrival of the migrating birds (although this is not true of the Lesser Celandine in England).

The **WINTER ACONITE** (*Eranthis hyemalis*), another member of the Buttercup family, is superficially similar to the Lesser Celandine. Originally native to central Europe, it flowers early in the year, sometimes alongside **SNOWDROPS** (*below*). It should not be confused with *Aconitum spp.*, Monk's-Hood (*see Poisonous Plants, pp. 56–57*).

**COMMON SNOWDROP** (*Galanthus nivalis*) takes its name from both the colour and shape of the flower and the fact that it often blooms while snow is still on the ground. However, the name is not ancient; it has also been known as **DEWDROP**, **DROOPING BELL**, **EVE'S TEAR**, **FEBRUARY FAIR MAIDS**, **WHITE BELLS** and even, in 1659 as "Early White Kind of Bulbous Violet".

Snowdrop

Lesser Celandine

Greater Celandine

ABOVE: **LESSER CELANDINE** *is one of our earliest wild flowers. Common in hedgerows, its bright star-like flowers herald the approach of spring, and provide nectar and pollen for bumblebees emerging from hibernation. It has been called* **PILEWORT** *because its small fleshy roots resemble an attack of piles.*

ABOVE: **GREATER CELANDINE** *is unrelated to Lesser Celendine. A tincture prepared from it was used in eye drops. A yellow sap from the stem of the same plant was used in the treatment of warts, hence its name* **WARTWORT** *in Somerset and Wiltshire.*

Winter Aconite

Winter Heliotrope

ABOVE: *The yellow flowers of* **WINTER ACONITE** *are sometimes mistaken for those of Lesser Celandine (top).*

ABOVE: **WINTER HELIOTROPE** (*Petasites pyranaicus*), *naturalised in Britain, bears pale mauve-pink scented flowers in winter months.*

# PAINTING THE MEADOWS
## *cuckoo flowers & buttercups*

---

**MILKMAIDS** (*Cardamine pratensis*) is a lovely spring flower with delicate pinkish-mauve petals. They look almost white in sunshine, perhaps to reflect the complexion of girls who milked cows in the meadows where it grows. It was also called **CUCKOO FLOWER**, according to Gerard, as it flowers '*… in Aprill and May, when the Cuckoo begins to sing her pleasant note …*'.    Another name, common across many English counties and still much used today, is **LADY'S SMOCK**, originally just **SMOCK**. In the seventeenth century, however, 'smock' had an unfortunate connotation, like the slang 'a piece of skirt'.

This indelicate name may have become Christianised as 'Our Lady's Smock'. Gerard adopted it: '*At Namptwich in Cheshire, where I had my beginning, [the name is] Ladie Smockes, which hath given me cause to Christen it after my Country fashion*'. It was taken up by Shakespeare in a song in *Loves Labours Lost* (with a hint of the association of cuckoos with adultery):

"*… lady-smocks all silver-white*
*And cuckoo-buds of yellow hue*
*Do paint the meadows with delight,*
*The cuckoo then, on every tree,*
*Mocks married men; for thus sings he,*
*Cuckoo*"

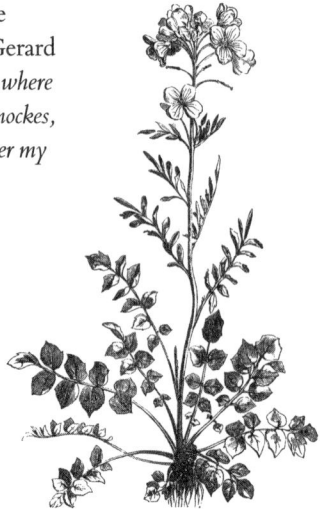

Lady's Smock

Buttercup

LEFT: **BUTTERCUPS** (Ranunculus spp.) were called 'cuckoo-buds' by Shakespeare. The name connects the cup-shaped yellow flowers and the colour of the butter produced by the cows which graze there (although cows don't eat the plants as they have an acrid flavour). It is said that if you hold a Buttercup under a small child's chin and the colour reflects there, which it does on a sunny day, it proves that the child likes butter!

BELOW: Several water-dwelling species of Ranunculus are called **WATER CROWFOOTS**, after the likeness of the finely divided underwater leaf to a crow's foot. Some of them have more rounded floating leaves, while the white flowers emerge above the surface. The Crowfoots lack the acrid flavour, thus they were once gathered by boat as cattle fodder.

Water Crowfoot

Yellow Water Lily

LEFT: **YELLOW WATER-LILY** (Nuphar lutea) is another native British water-dwelling plant, member of a primitive family. With rhizomes in the mud, it has large floating leaves and long-stalked yellow flowers. In several southern counties it is known as **BRANDY BOTTLE**, due to the winey smell of the flowers and the shape of its seed case.

# FLOWERS FROM THE BARD
### *daisies, violets & pansies*

---

"*When daisies pied and violets blue …*", wrote Shakespeare in *Loves Labours Lost* (*preceding his lines on lady-smocks, see previous page*).

The **DAISY** (*Bellis perennis*) is one of our commonest and most recognised flowers, and the bane of gardeners who prefer a pristine lawn. Its name derives from Anglo-Saxon *daeges-eage*, the 'eye of the day', a white flower which opens in daylight and whose yellow centre represents the sun. Chaucer referred to it thus: '*Wel by reson men hit calle may | The 'dayesye' or elles the 'ye of day' | The emperice and flour of flours alle.*'

The name **VIOLET** comes from early French and ultimately from the Latin *viola*. John Gerard, normally more concerned with the 'vertues' of plants, enthused about the beauty of violets: '*… their beautie, variety of colour and exquisite forme … delightfull to looke on, and pleasant to smell…*'.

The **DOG VIOLET** (*Viola riviniana*), is commoner than the **SWEET VIOLET**, and lacks its pleasant scent. As Grigson wrote, '*dog and horse are common English prefixes to distinguish an inferior species from its superior relative*'. The lovely hedge-scrambling pale pink **DOG ROSE** (*Rosa canina*) is named for its supposed inferiority to garden roses. Pliny wrote that the root of Dog Rose (*cynorrhodon*) cured hydrophobia. It is known as **CUCKOO'S SHOE** in Shropshire.

Daisy

Sweet Violet        Dog Violet        Dog Rose

*ABOVE: Violets are mentioned 18 times in Shakespeare's plays, often referring to the rapid fading of the scent of the* **SWEET VIOLET** *(Viola odorata). In Hamlet, Laertes tries to warn his sister Ophelia off the young Prince: "A violet in the youth of primy nature | Forward, not permanent, sweet, not lasting | The perfume and suppliance of a minute | No more."*

*LEFT:* **WHITE CLOVER** *(Trifolium repens) provides more nectar to UK insects than any other species, making it the favourite plant for bees. Shakespeare called it* **HONEYSTALKS** *as sweetness can be sucked from the flowers. Clover is an ancient word, the plant having similar names in other languages.*

White Clover

Wild Pansy

*LEFT:* **WILD PANSY** *(Viola tricolor) is also known as* **HEART'S-EASE** *and* **LOVE-IN-IDLENESS**, *perhaps from the idea that its two facing petals represent lovers about to kiss. Pansy comes from the French pensée, 'thought'. In A Midsummer Night's Dream, this 'little Western flower' is used by Oberon as a love potion.*

29

# PRIVATE PLANTS
### orchids & wild arum

EARLY PURPLE ORCHID (*Orchis mascula*) is one of our commonest wild orchids, sometimes growing in profusion on chalk downland. Named for its colour and season, it also has many colourful local English names, such as SAMMY GUSSETS in Somerset and GRAMFER-GRIDDLE-GOOSEY-GANDER in Wiltshire. Shakespeare may have been referring to this plant in *Hamlet* when describing the garlands held by drowning Ophelia '*… long purples | That liberal shepherds give a grosser name | But our cold maids do dead men's fingers call them*'. However, Shakespeare learnt his wild flower names in Warwickshire, where LONG PURPLES and DEAD MEN'S FINGERS were local names for WILD ARUM.

Both these flowers have many much 'grosser' local names. The name DOG'S STONES (testicles) was applied to both in different areas, while the Wild Arum was called CUCKOO-PINT (shortened from CUCKOO'S PINTLE) and PARSON-IN-THE-PULPIT (from PARSON'S PINTLE). 'Pintle' was an old word for the male organ. The polite name LORDS-AND-LADIES, commonly used today, was deliberately invented to replace the older and more indecent ones.

Wild Arum

*RIGHT:* **BEE ORCHID** (Ophrys apifera). *The flower is intricately patterned in shades of brownish-red, yellow and pink. It so resembles a bumblebee, with the scent of a female, that males attempt to mate with it, ensuring the plant's pollination. The less-common* **FLY ORCHID** *(O. insectifera) has a flower with a shiny area, mimicking the wings of small insects. Orchids have distinctive paired tubers. The word comes from orkhis, the Greek for testicle. One tuber shrinks as it feeds the young plant. Later in the season, its partner expands to store food from the leaves. Preparations from the expanding tuber were said to increase sexual desire, the shrinking tuber to decrease it, a practice first recorded by Dioscorides.*

Bee
Orchid

Fly
Orchid

Early
Purple
Orchid

*LEFT:* **EARLY PURPLE ORCHID** *is found throughout Britain and has a large number of paired local names, like* **ADAM AND EVE**, **CAIN AND ABEL** *or* **DUCKS AND DRAKES**, *suggesting that its tubers were well-known and much used.*

*FACING PAGE:* **WILD ARUM**. *Its upstanding spadix of minute flowers is enclosed by a spathe, the whole looking like a sexual symbol. The tubers of the plant were therefore consumed as an aphrodisiac.*

31

# COURTSHIP FLOWERS
## *forget-me-not & mistletoe*

---

**WATER FORGET-ME-NOT** (*Myosotis scorpioides*) blooms beside rivers, streams, lakes and ponds from May to September. Some local names, such as **BIRD'S EYE** (Somerset) and **ROBIN'S EYE** (Hampshire) refer to the central yellow star or 'eye' within each blue flower. Gerard named it **SCORPION GRASS** from its curled opening inflorescence. Samuel Taylor Coleridge introduced the name into English from the German in his 1802 poem, *The Keepsake*:

> *Nor can I find, amid my lonely walk*
> *By rivulet, or spring, or wet roadside*
> *That blue and bright-eyed flowerlet of the brook,*
> *Hope's gentle gem, the sweet forget-me-not!*

Another English plant name deriving from German is **COMMON TOADFLAX** (*Linaria vulgaris*), translated from *krottenflax* by William Turner in 1548. The second part of the name is due to the plant's flax-like leaves. Various theories have been put forward for the link with toads. The most likely is that it comes from the wide 'mouth' of the yellow flower. It is also sometimes referred to as **WILD SNAPDRAGON**. **IVY-LEAVED TOADFLAX** (*Cymbalaria muralis, shown facing*), which scrambles over walls, is related to Common Toadflax, having flowers of a similar shape, although its name is a contradiction in terms.

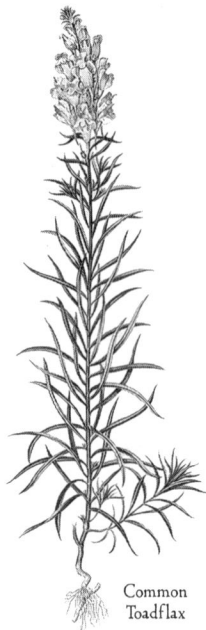

Common
Toadflax

Forget-
Me-Not

Mistletoe

ABOVE: **MISTLETOE** (Viscum album) was
'mistel-tan' in Old English, meaning 'different
twig' – as it looks different to the tree on which
it feeds. Sacred to the Viking goddess of love,
Frigga, we still kiss under her mistletoe today.

ABOVE: **FORGET-ME-NOT**: Legend tells how a
knight and lady were walking by a stream when
she saw some flowers on the opposite bank. He
swam across and picked them for her; but as he
returned, the current swept him away. Before he
died he threw her the flowers and cried out in
Middle High German – 'vergisz mein nicht'.

Periwinkle

Ivy-leaved
Toadflax

ABOVE: **PERIWINKLES** (Vinca major and
V. minor) derive their name, via Old English,
from Pliny's vinca pervinca, meaning 'conquer
to bind and entwine'. Medieval preparations of
'Pervinca powdered with earthworms' were
said to induce love between husband and wife!

# NETTLES & DOCKS
*the sting and its relief*

---

If there is one wild plant which is almost universally recognised, it must be the **COMMON NETTLE** (*Urtica dioica*). More familiarly known as the **STINGING NETTLE**, it grows best on disturbed ground and so is often found near human habitations – even if long abandoned.

The word 'nettle' goes back to Old English and may relate to the use of its fibrous stems in making fabrics. With suitable preparation, the leaves can be used in salads and are also used to make nettle soup.

Its sting is an effective defence against grazing animals and produces an irritating rash on human skin. The plant, especially the lower sides of leaves, is covered with special hairs called spicules. When brushed against, each acts like a tiny hypodermic syringe, injecting formic acid and other chemicals. If the plant is grasped firmly, the hairs tend to be pushed flat thus avoiding penetrating the skin. This is the origin of the expression '*to grasp the nettle*'; to tackle a difficult problem boldly.

Common Nettle

Other plants have leaves very similar to nettle leaves, but with no sting. The **WHITE DEADNETTLE** (*Lamium album*) is a common wayside flower, with whorls of flowers which are attractive to bees.

Yellow
Archangel

White
Deadnettle

Red
Dead
nettle

*ABOVE:* **YELLOW ARCHANGEL** (Lamiastrum galeobdolon) *is similar to* **WHITE DEADNETTLE** (Lamium album)*. Its intricately patterned flowers appear in woodland alongside bluebells. In the Middle Ages most members of the deadnettle family, including* **RED DEADNETTLE** (Lamium purpureum)*, were called* **ARCHANGELICA***, perhaps indicating their lack of an unpleasant sting. Around the Malvern Hills, Yellow Archangel was known as* **YELLOW WEASEL-SNOUT***, for* **GALEOBDOLON** *means 'smelling like a weasel' (when its leaves are crushed).*
*BELOW: An antidote to nettle stings is often found growing nearby. Leaves of the* **BROAD-LEAVED DOCK** (Rumex obtusifolius, below) *applied to the skin rapidly soothe the sting.*

Curled Dock

Small Dock

Broad Leaved Dock

# BURRS & CLEAVERS
### *and cow parsley too*

---

After a country walk you may need to disentangle burrs from your dog's coat or from your own clothing. In 1948, George de Mestral was inspired to invent Velcro fastening after examining the sharp hooks on Burdock seed-cases through a microscope. In some European languages, the same word serves for both 'velcro' and 'burdock'. The commonest British species is **LESSER BURDOCK** (*Arctium minus, see below*).

Burdock roots and leaves are eaten, mostly in the Far East. Oil extracted from Burdock roots is used as a scalp treatment. A medieval Dandelion and Burdock beverage was made from fermented roots, but the modern form is generally not based on plant material.

Another common plant which distributes its seeds by 'cleaving' on clothes or fur is **CLEAVERS** (*Galium aparine, opposite top left*), also known as **STICKY WILLY, CLAGGY MEGGIES, GOOSE-GRASS** (as poultry like it) or **KISSES** or **SWEETHEARTS** as they can be counted on friends' clothes and used to tease them about their number of boyfriends or girlfriends.

Greater Burdock

Lesser Burdock

Cleavers

Cow Parsley

Butterbur

ABOVE: **COW PARSLEY** (Anthriscus sylvestris), or Queen Anne's Lace. Its leaves make good food for pet rabbits. In Somerset it was called 'eltrot'. The word 'parsley' derives, via French and Latin, from the Greek petros and selinon, meaning 'rock celery'. 'Cow' comes from its inferior quality, or from its habitat along lanes and cow-paths.

LEFT: Just as Burdock is partly named from the similarity of its leaves to those of Dock, so **BUTTERBUR** (Petasites hybridus) is named for its slight similarity to Burdock, although it does not produce burrs. Large Butterbur leaves were once used by farmers' wives to wrap home-made butter for market.

37

# GONE WITH THE WIND
*as light as thistledown*

---

Twenty-eight species of prickly plants, members of seven different genera, are known as **THISTLES** in Britain. The Anglo-Saxon word *thistel* seems to derive from even earlier languages. Their light-weight seeds, called thistledown, can be blown many miles by the wind. Other plants similarly use fluffy seeds for wide dispersal.

A single tall pink-flowered spike of **ROSEBAY WILLOWHERB** (*Chamerion angustifolium*) can produce 80,000 seeds, which germinate well on burnt ground. A scarce plant in the mid-nineteenth century, it took advantage of the developing railway network. Its seeds, wafted in the slipstreams of steam trains, germinated where sparks had burnt embankments, and it is now common throughout Britain. 'Rosebay' was invented by Turner, while 'Willowherb' comes from the similarity of the leaves to those of willow. Its American name, **FIREWEED**, may have been taken across the Atlantic by emigrants from Dorset.

Common Sow Thistle      Musk Thistle      Rosebay Willowherb

Ox-Eye
Daisy

LEFT: *The striking white flowers of* **OX-EYE DAISY** (Leucanthemum vulgare) *are frequently seen on the verges of motorways. Like Rosebay and Ragwort, its numerous light seeds are spread by slipstreams, in this case of road traffic. It obtained its name by translation from the Greek bouphthalmon. It was once known as the* **WHITE OX-EYE** *to distinguish it from the Yellow Ox-eye or Corn Marigold (see page 1). Today bouphthalmos is a medical term for an enlarged eye-ball.*

RIGHT: **OXFORD RAGWORT** (Senecio squalidus) *was growing in Oxford Botanic Garden by the 1770s, brought from the slopes of Mount Etna in Sicily. Within 60 years its bright yellow flowers could be seen at Oxford railway station. From there the draught from passing trains transported the seeds, which found the gravel of the railway track a good substitute for volcanic lava. Both Oxford and* **COMMON RAGWORT** (Senecio jacobaea) *are poisonous to horses and cattle, especially if accidentally incorporated into hay. The name refers to the 'ragged' leaves. Known as* **STINKING WILLIE** *in Wales, ragwort is the food plant of the black-and-yellow-striped caterpillars of the Cinnabar Moth* (Tyria jacobaeae).

Ragwort

# THE FINE ART OF FORAGING
*the bounty of nature*

––––––––––––

The carrots which we grow in our gardens derive from purple-rooted Asian ancestors, not from the **WILD CARROT** (*Daucus carota*) of British calcareous grassland. The name derives from *karoton*, the Greek name for the plant. On the other hand, the yellow-umbelled **WILD PARSNIP** (*Pastinaca sativa*) is closely related to the cultivated variety; its wiry roots are just about edible. 'Parsnip' and the generic name are related to the Latin verb *pastinare*, to dig.

**FAT HEN** (*Chenopodium album*) and the closely-related **GOOD-KING-HENRY** (*C. bonus-henricus*) provided food from prehistoric times, the leaves being used like spinach. The oily seeds of Fat Hen ('Hen' short for 'Henry') were part of the last meal of Tollund Man; a preserved Iron Age body excavated from a Danish Bog.

**SALAD BURNET** (*Poterium sanguisorba*) smells of cucumber when crushed and its young leaves were used in salads. 'Burnet' is adopted from a related species with mahogany-coloured flowers, while the specific name relates its herbal use in staunching wounds.

**RAMSONS** or **WILD GARLIC** (*Allium ursinum*) was used in cooking in the past and both its names are Old English. *Garleac* was the 'spear-leek', while *hramsa* referred to the plant's rank smell. John Evelyn, the 17th-century diarist, wrote: '*Tis not for ladies' palates – nor for those who court them*'!

Ramsons

40

Wild Carrot                    Wild Parsnip                    Sea Kale

ABOVE: *Some wild staples.* **SEA KALE** *(Crambe maritima) is a delicious wild Brassica, with white flowers. Its cousin, the yellow-flowering* **WILD CABBAGE** *(Brassica oleracea, shown on page 58) grows on coastal cliffs. 'Cabbage' comes from the Old French* caboche, *'head'.*

Fat Hen                        Good King Henry                Salad Burnet

ABOVE: *Delicious greens.* LEFT: **FAT HEN** *is a shortened form of Fat Henry. It has also been called* **PIGWEED** *and* **DIRTY DICK**. CENTRE: **GOOD KING HENRY** *takes its name from Guter Heinrich, a German goblin-herbalist. Gerard added 'King' to the translation. It is also known as* **MERCURY** *after the Roman god.* RIGHT: **SALAD BURNET** *was* **POOR MAN'S PEPPER** *in Dorset.*

# NATURE'S PHARMOCOPOEIA
*treating conditions of heart, head and eye*

---

**MEADOWSWEET** (*Filipendula ulmaria* formerly *Spiraea ulmaria*) is a source of salicylic acid, the active ingredient in aspirin (whose name was coined from Spiraea), and has been used to treat headaches. It is also called **QUEEN OF THE MEADOWS** in many English counties, and **MEAD WORT**, as it was used to flavour mead. When homes had floors of stone or earth, Meadowsweet was the favourite 'strewing herb', used to soften the surface and provide a sweet and pleasant smell.

**FOXGLOVE** (*Digitalis purpurea*), from the medieval *'foxes glofa'*, is a statuesque plant of woodlands. Generations of children have enjoyed fitting its mottled purple flowers onto their fingers. It has long been used to treat conditions of the heart (*see opposite*). Other names include **FAIRY GLOVES** and **LADY'S THIMBLE**.

**EYEBRIGHT** (*Euphrasia spp.*) is a small grassland plant. In 1657, William Coles noted that its little white flowers have '… *purple and yellow spots and stripes (which) doth very much resemble the diseases of the eye …*'. This is why, due to the Doctrine of Signatures, Eyebright preparations have long been used to treat the eyes. In Milton's *'Paradise Lost'*, Archangel Michael clears Adam's vision by the use of Euphrasie (Eyebright) – '… *purg'd with euphrasie and rue the visual nerve, for he had much to see*'.

Eyebright

Meadowsweet

Foxglove

Wild Marjoram

Great Mullein

ABOVE: Nature's pharmacy. **MEADOWSWEET**, like willow bark, contains salicylic acid, a natural painkiller. Infusions of **FOXGLOVE** leaves had long been used as a treatment for dropsy, when in 1785, William Withering showed that the main effect was on the heart, and that an exact dose of dried leaf was critical (too many natural toxins from the leaves can be fatal). **WILD MARJORAM** (Origanum vulgare) once had a reputation as a herbal cure-all.

LEFT: **GREAT MULLEIN** (Verbascum thapsus) was called **DONKEY'S EAR** in Dorset from the woolly hairs on its leaves. Preparations from roots, stems and leaves were prescribed not only for humans but also for lung diseases in cattle.

# HEALING PLANTS
## *from Comfrey to Yarrow*

---

**COMMON COMFREY** (*Symphytum officinale*) derives its name from Latin *confervere*, to grow together, and has been called **KNITBONE** in English. If the roots are grated, made into a mash and applied with lint to a broken limb, the preparation contracts, pulling the wound together. Comfrey has been proved to promote the healing of bruises. Also, its leaves can be infused to make a (smelly) tomato fertiliser.

**RIBWORT PLANTAIN** (*Plantago lanceolata*) is named from *planta*, the sole of the foot. As plantain survives bruising on well-trodden grassy paths, it must heal bruised skin! In *Romeo and Juliet*, Romeo recommends treatment for Benvolio's injury: *'Your plantain-leaf is excellent for that'* | *'For what, I pray thee?'* | *'For your broken shin'*. In North America, the indigenous peoples called it **WHITE MAN'S FOOT** as it spread wherever the settlers travelled.

**YARROW** (*Achillea millefolium*) was *gearwe* in Old English, signifying its healing properties. Achilles used Yarrow to heal wounds during the Trojan war, hence the generic name *Achillea*; the Roman legions used it to treat bleeding.

**VIPER'S BUGLOSS** (*Echium vulgare*), also known as **SNAKE FLOWER**, or **BLUE DEVIL**, was equated by Renaissance herbalists with a plant which Dioscorides recommended as a cure for snake bite, as its seed-case resembles a viper's head. Its rough leaves give its name Bugloss, from the Greek *bouglossos*, ox-tongue.

Viper's
Bugloss

Comfrey

Plantain

Yarrow

Common Scurvy Grass

Betony

Nipplewort

*ABOVE:* **COMMON SCURVY-GRASS** (Cochlearia officinalis) *is a coastal plant, proposed as a cure for scurvy by Dodoens in 1553. This disease, caused by a lack of vitamin C, was once common on long sea voyages.* **BETONY** (Stachys officinalis) *was named* vettonica *by Pliny after the Spanish Vettones tribe, who he said discovered its many herbal uses, from digestive to breathing problems.* **NIPPLEWORT** (Lapsana communis) *has buds which look a little like nipples, which led German apothecaries to apply preparations for cracked and ulcerated nipples. The German name passed into English. An infusion staunches the flow of breast milk.*

# PLANTS NAMED FOR USES
*more herbal remedies*

---

Traditional herbal cures have been used for centuries. Even today, medical herbalists prepare plant parts as creams and ointments for external use and as infusions, syrups and cordials for internal use.

**SAGE** tea has long been thought to improve memory. Research shows that it may slow the progress of Alzheimer's disease.

**GREATER STITCHWORT** (*Stellaria holostea*) had 'worth' as an antidote for 'stitch' or muscle cramps. It was drunk '*... in wine with the powder of acorns ...*' according to Gerard. Unlike many classically-derived names, Stitchwort is a native name from at least as long ago as the 13th century.

**SELF-HEAL** (*Prunella vulgaris*) has substances in its leaves that sooth cuts and bruises, and was widely used as a gargle. According to a French saying, '*no-one wants a surgeon who keeps Prunelle*'.

**TORMENTIL** (*Potentilla erecta*) – the 'little torment plant' – its roots boiled in milk were used to treat severe stomach pains or toothache. It was also used in the Scottish islands for tanning leather, as it contains, weight for weight, seven times as much tannin as oak bark.

Stitchwort      Self-heal      Tormentil

**WOOD SAGE** (Teucrium scorodonia) *is a tall plant with small yellowish-green flowers. Used as a diuretic, or as a treatment for rheumatism.*

**GARLIC MUSTARD** (Alliaria petiolata), *or* **SAUCE-ALONE**, *was used as a condiment, esp. with salt fish. White flowers. Also known as* **JACK-BY-THE-HEDGE**, *where it is found.*

**SQUINANCYWORT** (Asperula cynanchica) *grows on chalk grassland, especially on old ant heaps. It was used as a gargle against squinancy, or quincy, a throat infection.*

**TEASEL** (Dipsacus fullonum). *The dried seed heads, with their fine hooked spikes, were used in the weaving process to 'tease' or 'nap' the texture of cloth.*

**FLEABANE** (Pulicaria dysenterica) *has intensely yellow composite flowers. It is related to, and smells of, Chrysanthemum, the basis of pyrethrum insecticide (made from the seed cases). The smoke of the dried leaves fumigated a flea-infested cottage, while hung bunches were a preventative.*

# CORNFIELDS AND CLOCKS
*chequered boxes and a horse's footprint*

---

**COMMON POPPY** (*Papaver rhoeas*): the word 'poppy' can be traced all the way back to 'pa-pa' in the Sumerian of Ur in the 4th century BC. As Neolithic farming spread the growing of corn from the Middle East to Northern Europe, so the weed and variations on its name followed. One poppy can produce 17,000 seeds, some of which can remain dormant for over 40 years. As a result there are sometimes spectacular scarlet displays on newly disturbed ground.

**COMMON RESTHARROW** (*Ononis repens*) is a low-growing plant with pink pea-flowers, formerly considered a weed in arable fields. A horse-drawn harrow, breaking up ploughed soil, could be stopped in its tracks ('brought to rest') when tangled in the long thick rhizomes, which were once chewed like liquorice.

Restharrow

Poppy

Moschatel

LEFT: **MOSCHATEL** (Adoxa moschatellina).
Its name comes from the Greek moskos,
meaning musk; when the tiny plant is wet, it
exudes a musky smell, hence another name
MUSKROOT. Its Cumberland name of TOWN
HALL CLOCK is also apt as the small green
flower-head has four flowers facing, as it were,
north, south, east and west; each with five
petals. A fifth flower faces directly upwards,
and remarkably, for the symmetry to work,
this has only four petals.

Fritillary

Coltsfoot

**FRITILLARY** (Fritillaria meleagris) has
petals patterned with mauve chequers. It is
named from Latin 'fritillus,' a dice-box. Also
known as SNAKE'S HEAD FRITILLARY it
makes a wondrous April display in the few
damp hay meadows where it survives.

**COLTSFOOT** (Tussilago farfara) has a large
leaf shaped like a horse's footprint, hence the
name. The flowers appear long before the
leaves, so it was once called SON-BEFORE-
THE-FATHER. Preparations from the leaves
and roots may be effective against coughs.

# CONNECTIONS WITH STORIES
## symbols and meaning

---

Just as a Bullfinch is a large finch, so '**BULRUSH**' implies a large rush. The name originally applied to the sedge *Schoenoplectus lacustris*, nowadays **COMMON CLUB-RUSH**, while the plant we now call Bulrush is *Typha latifolia*, the **GREAT REED-MACE** (as its spike resembles a mace-head).

The confusion arose from a popular Victorian illustration of '*Moses in the Bulrushes*' (though the plant growing by the Nile would have been Papyrus). This was supposedly due to a painting by Sir Lawrence Alma-Tadema, but he does not seem to have painted this subject. The roots of a stand of Reedmaces can be used to purify waste water.

**SHEPHERD'S-PURSE** (*Capsella bursa-pastoris*) is generally considered a common weed, as it produces vast quantities of seed and can have several generations in a growing season. It is named for its stalked seed-case, suggestive of a countryman's hanging purse, as seen in the 1567 painting *The Peasant Dance*, by Pieter Bruegel the Elder.

Shpherd's Purse

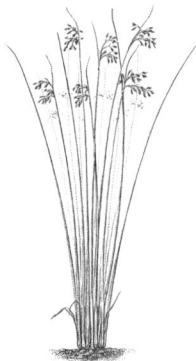

Club-rush

Bulrush

Bird's Foot Trefoil

Lady's Bedstraw

LEFT: **BIRD'S-FOOT-TREFOIL** (Lotus corniculatus) *is a low-growing plant which can colour whole areas of downland a rich golden-yellow for much of the summer. The name comes from its three-lobed leaf and the shape of the dry pods. Local names, such as* **DEVIL'S CLAWS**, *were replaced with the Christianised (Our)* **LADY'S FINGERS**.

**LADY'S BEDSTRAW** (Galium verum), *when dried, smells like new-mown hay and was once used in straw mattresses. Legend tells that Bedstraw was part of the bedding in the Bethlehem stable. To honour the birth of Christ, the plant blossomed, its tiny flowers changing from white to gold, giving the plant its name of (Our Blessed)* **LADY'S BEDSTRAW**.

RIGHT: **WATER MINT** (Mentha aquatica) *In Greek myth, Pluto took a fancy to the nymph Minthe. His partner Persephone crushed her rival underfoot changing her into an aromatic herb. Mint still gives off its best odour if trodden upon, therefore it was once used as a strewing herb. It has purple flowers and in Hampshire was called* **BISHOPSWEED**.

**COMMON CENTAURY** (Centaurium erythraea) *has deep pink flowers and takes its name from the half-man-half-horse of Greek myths. Chiron the centaur was considered knowledgeable in medicine. Legend tells that he taught Man the virtues of Centaury, and used it to heal a wound in his own foot, after dropping one of Hercules' arrows onto it.*

Water Mint

Centaury

# WOODY PLANTS AND SHRUBS
## *often found in hedgerows*

---

Many of the plants in this book are herbs in the sense that they may have medicinal or culinary uses. Almost all are herbs in the botanical sense—herbaceous plants, with no woody tissues in their stems. Of the non-herbaceous (woody) plants, a few shrubs are mentioned here.

**HAZEL** (*Corylus avellana*) grows in hedges and as an under-layer in woodland. Traditionally it was coppiced (cut back to base on a seven-year cycle) and the supple young branches used for wattle, hurdles and thatching spars. Its male flowers are catkins, sometimes called **LAMB'S TAILS**. The tiny red female flowers develop into hazel-nuts.

**HAWTHORN** (*Crataegus monogyna*) is a very common hedgerow shrub, named from its thorns and its berry-like haws. It is also called May. Before the Julian calendar was replaced by the Gregorian (in 1752 in Britain), it would have blossomed around May 1st, now it flowers in mid-May. The saying '*Ne'er cast a clout till May be out*' more likely refers to the opening of the flowers rather than to the end of the month.

Hazel

Hawthorn

Blackthorn          Gorse          Buddleja

Elder

**ELDER** (Sambucus nigra) is a straggly bush. The fruit is often used for country wine, while cordials can be prepared from the white flowers.

*ABOVE:* **BLACKTHORN** (Prunus spinosa) *fills spring hedgerows with drifts of snow-white flowers. A cold snap, often after a 'false spring,' is known as a blackthorn winter. It makes good spiny hedges and walking sticks, and the blue-black fruit,* **SLOES,** *are used for sloe wine and gin.*

**GORSE** (Ulex europaeus), *known as* **FURZE** *in the New Forest, has been used as fodder for animals and as fuel for ovens. Gorse always seems to sport some yellow flowers whatever the time of year, hence the saying 'when gorse is not in flower, kissing's out of season'.*

**BUDDLEJA** (B. davidii) *came from China in the 1890s. Grown as a decorative garden shrub, it has also taken over much waste land. Its purple flower-spikes are rich in nectar and can support large populations of butterflies, giving it the popular name of* **BUTTERFLY BUSH.**

# CLIMBING PLANTS
*upwards to the light*

---

Some climbers are woody, others are herbaceous. All take advantage of shrubs, trees and buildings to grow upwards. It is interesting that the names **IVY** and **BRAMBLE**, as well as **HOLLY**, **HAWTHORN**, **BLACKTHORN**, **SLOE**, **HAZEL**, **ELDER**, **GORSE** and **FURZE**, all originate at least as far back as Old English (before c.1100 AD).

**HONEYSUCKLE** (*Lonicera periclymenum*) is named for the sweetness that can be sucked from the flower. It produces its best scent at night to attract pollinating moths. **IVY** (*Hedera helix*) is a woody climber that can cover trees and ruins. Its flowers are important to insects late in the year. Along with **HOLLY** (*Ilex aquifolium*), it has a traditional evergreen link to Christmas, transferred from former pagan folklore. Shakespeare used Ivy and Honeysuckle together in *A Midsummer Night's Dream* as plant similes for lovers entwined:

> *So doth the woodbine the sweet honeysuckle*
> *Gently entwist; the female ivy so*
> *Enrings the barky fingers of the elm.*
> *O, how I love thee!*

Honeysuckle

Holly

Ivy

Horseshoe Vetch

LEFT: **HORSESHOE VETCH** (Anthyllis comosa) There are around eight species of Vetch found in Britain, members of the pea family. 'Vetch' comes from Old Norman French veche, referring to their scrambling habit. The more common **KIDNEY VETCH** is named after the shape of its lower leaves.

BELOW: **BRAMBLE / BLACKBERRY** (Rubus 'fruticosus') has spiny looping stems which can climb or form a thicket. Gathering blackberries remains a popular form of foraging. It is said that the berries should not be picked after Old Michaelmas Day, Sept 29th, when the devil spits on them.

**FIELD BINDWEED** (Convolvulus arvensis) The pink-and-white flowered Field Bindweed is the true convolvulus, taking its scientific name from the Latin convolvo – I intertwine. The alternative name **CORNBINE** also refers to its habit of scrambling over other plants. The larger white flowers of the **HEDGE BINDWEED** (Calystegia sepium) are often, incorrectly, referred to in English as Convolvulus. Old local names include **LADY'S NIGHTCAP** and **WITHYWIND**.

Bramble

Field Bindweed

# POISONOUS PLANTS
*how deadly is nightshade?*

---

Among the innocent plants of the British countryside, there are a number that could be fatal, so should be treated with respect.

**DEADLY NIGHTSHADE** (*Atropa belladonna*) has dangling purple flowers which develop into black berries. All parts of the plant are poisonous, the berries particularly so. A child can die after eating two or three, ten to twenty can kill an adult. In 16th century Venice a dilute preparation was used as a cosmetic, supposedly making a lady more beautiful by enlarging the pupils of her eyes – hence 'belladonna'.

**WOODY NIGHTSHADE** (*Solanum dulcamara*) scrambles through hedgerows and is often confused with Deadly Nightshade, but its berries are not black, nor deadly. An alternative name is **BITTERSWEET**. Tomatoes and Potatoes are also members of the genus *Solanum*.

**ENCHANTER'S-NIGHTSHADE** (*Circaea lutetiana*) is doubly misnamed. It is a member of the Willowherb family, so not really a Nightshade and it has no real association with 'enchanters'.

Deadly Nightshade        Woody Nightshade        Enchanter's Nightshade

Hemlock

LEFT: **HEMLOCK WATER DROPWORT** (Oenanthe crocata) *is a tall plant similar to Cow Parsley, but with purple-blotched stems and an unpleasant smell (said to resemble mouse urine!). It is harmful to horses and cattle, giving rise to the Yorkshire name of* COWBANE; *while the roots have been called* DEAD MEN'S FINGERS. *All parts of the plant are poisonous to humans and consuming only a morsel can prove fatal.*

RIGHT: **MONK'S-HOOD** (Aconitum napellus) *has flowers like small blue helmets. Other names like* DEVIL'S HELMET *suggest its poisonous nature. All parts are harmful, especially the roots, and can be fatal, but cases are rare due to an unpleasant flavour. It should be handled with care as toxins can enter the blood through cuts. Related species have been used to poison the tips of arrows.*

Monk's Hood

Dog's Mercury

LEFT: **DOG'S MERCURY** (Mercurialis perennis) *is a small all-green plant which can spread over large areas of a woodland floor. As always, 'Dog' is pejorative in a plant name. Unlike the 'true' Mercuries (Chenopodium species such as Good-King-Henry, p.41), Dog's Mercury is highly poisonous. Ingestion of this plant can lead to vomiting, jaundice, coma and eventually death.*

# CARING FOR WILD FLOWERS

For children growing up in the countryside from prehistoric times until relatively recently it was second nature to know the names of all the common wild flowers. They were to be found everywhere—from arable fields to bleak moorland, from the sea coast to mountain crags, in the woods and in the meadows. In some places they still thrive.

However, over recent decades, cities, towns and villages have expanded into the countryside, and modern agriculture has resulted in the removal of many miles of hedgerows, the draining of flower-carpeted water meadows and the extensive use of herbicides.

To stem the tide of destruction, conservation bodies, official and charitable, attempt to maintain the biodiversity of our wild flora in nature reserves, while encouraging landowners and the public to care for the treasures of our countryside—we all have a part to play.

*THE PICTURES IN THIS BOOK have been drawn from a wide variety of sources. Many have been taken from Gerard's 1484-page* Herball, *published in 1597. A large number come from Rev C A John's 'Flowers of the Field' (34th edition of 1919 – first published in 1853). Line drawings in this volume were by John's sisters Julia and Emily while half-tone illustrations were taken from water-colours by Emily Stackhouse, an eminent Victorian botanical artist. Other images are from* Herbarius Latinus, *Peter Schoeffer, 1484;* Buch der Natur, *Conrad Megenberg, 1475;* Phytognomonica, *Giambattista Porta, 1588;* Botanicum Medicale, *J. Millan, 1768;* Flora Londinensis, *William Curtis, 1777;* Botanical Magazine, *1800-1948; and herbals by Peter Treveris, 1526; Friedrich Hayne, pub. 1805-1846; Jan Kops, pub. 1800-1920. J. Roques, 1821 & 1825; Hermann Köhler, 1887 & 1890; Willibald Artus, 1846 & 1855; Alfred Bennett & George Murray, 1889; Frederick Hulme, 1890; William Drury, 1900; Charles Garola, 1904; F. Losch, 1914. The standard English and Linnaean names are as used in* Collins Wild Flower Guide *(2016 edition) with some scientific names changed to reflect current usage.*

Wild Cabbage (p.41)